Confessions for WAITING PARENTS

A 40-Day Devotional Journey for Expectant Couples

'TOYE & 'KIITAN **OYEDUN**

REVIEW AND TESTIMONIAL

Confessions For Waiting Parents - A 40-Day Devotional Journey for Expectant Couples - This is a must-read devotional for every waiting couple- it is uplifting and encouraging. I like the fact that every day reminds us of the promise of God regarding fruitfulness that never fails. It's simple and easy to read, yet so powerful and encouraging that I was almost tempted to read everything in a sitting. I pray this will inspire every waiting couple as they trust God to embrace their miracle babies in Jesus mighty name.

... Pastor Ekaete Adejumobi

****

I first heard about Aunty Kiitan even before I moved to Canada, and though we weren't close then, I felt drawn to her.

In 2023, she reached out and suggested we pray together weekly, even if only for 10 minutes. She would call faithfully, encourage me, and pray with me even on days when I didn't feel like praying. Her kindness and persistence carried me through many low moments.

When difficult doctors' reports came, she would always give me a scripture and pray against the negative words.

One morning, she sent me a message saying, **"It is done. God told me to tell you, and you should rejoice evermore."** About a couple of weeks later, God confirmed that word in my life; it was truly done!

That is why this devotional is so dear to my heart. I have experienced firsthand the faith, scriptures, and prayers that Aunty Kiitan now shares in these pages. This is more than a book. it is a companion for waiting parents, filled with the same hope and encouragement that carried me through my own journey.

… MF. A.

****

It was just like yesterday, when Pastor Kiitan walked up to me, asked if I wouldn't mind if she joined me and my husband in prayer for the fruit of the womb, which I agreed to. It was really surprising to me, seeing a pastor with so much humility and passion, willing to go all out for my husband and I.

We began our weekly prayer journey. She was more dedicated to the prayer session than I was because I was already losing hope due to my husband's carefree nature about giving birth.

When we had our first issue, which we lost, it made me start doubting God. Pastor Kiitan's unwavering faith, wisdom, and dedication kept me going; her encouragement, prayers, and constant follow-up kept me afloat.

The week I was to take the pregnancy test, she told my husband that "the word of the Lord will be confirmed in our life" On the Thursday of the same week, I confirmed I was pregnant.

I am a living testimony of God's answered prayer, and truly, He set people around us to lift us up when we grow weak and weary, and that's why this devotional is exciting to me, as it outlines some of the prayers we prayed through the period.

Pastor Kiitan was a divine helper sent to me and my family.

… TR.O.

****

Now I know for certain that God never intended for us to walk this journey of life alone. One day, Pastor Kiitan walked up to me in church and said she felt led to join me in prayers for the fruit of the womb. She even added, with such humility, that I should feel free to tell her to mind her own business if I was uncomfortable or felt she was overreaching. That lack of inhibition and the purity of her approach caught my attention, and from there began a weekly prayer journey that changed my life.

Through every session, Pastor Kiitan's long-suffering, unwavering faith, sage-like wisdom, and heartfelt candour endeared her to me, even during times when I wasn't consistent in showing up. She didn't just pray with me, she taught me to internalise scriptures and cling to God's promises concerning fruitfulness and motherhood.

Then came the defining moment. Just a week before I took the pregnancy test that confirmed I was indeed pregnant, she sent me a simple but weighty text: "The word of the Lord has been confirmed concerning you and yours in Jesus' name. Rejoice forever." There was something so thick, so alive in that message. It felt different somehow. And true to His word, God watched over His promise and speedily performed it in my life.

I stand today as a living testimony that God is faithful, God hears, God answers, and God remembers. Truly, He sets people around us to lift us when our hands grow weary, and for me, Pastor Kiitan was one of those divinely sent helpers.

… ET. B.

CONFESSIONS FOR WAITING PARENTS

Published by Cornerstone Publishing

A Division of Cornerstone Creativity Group LLC
Info@thecornerstonepublishers.com
www.thecornerstonepublishers.com

Author's Contact

To book the author to speak at your next event or to order bulk copies of this book, please, use the information below:

authors@crescitebooks.com

For Crescite Books updates and notification about upcoming books, reach out to:

info@crescitebooks.com

Printed in the United States of America.

FOREWORD

Having read *Confessions for Waiting Parents – A 40 Day Devotional Journey for Expectant Couples*, we can confidently say that this book is a powerful tool for anyone trusting God for the glorious testimony of childbirth.

Each page carries more than words; it carries hope, faith, and divine assurance. The declarations are filled with life-giving power, the testimonies are deeply encouraging, and the scriptures backing each confession resonate profoundly with the heart of anyone in the waiting season. It's not just a book; it's a daily encounter with God's promises concerning fruitfulness.

We believe this devotional will help shape your mindset, strengthen your spirit, and align your words with God's will during this sacred journey. Whether you are believing for your first child or trusting God again after loss or delay, this book will keep your heart anchored in truth.

We encourage you not only to read it but to internalise the words and meditate on them daily. Speak the declarations out loud. Let them become the atmosphere of your heart and home.

And don't keep this gift to yourself, share it. Buy copies for friends, family, and loved ones who are in their waiting season. Let this devotional be the seed that births many testimonies.

This book is a blessing, and we pray it brings forth abundant fruit in your life.

With love and faith,
Sola & Nike Ajayi
Realm Academy For Family Life
www.realmacademyforfamilylife.com

CONTENTS

PREFACE

This devotional is lovingly crafted for expectant parents who find themselves waiting with hope and faith. Whether you are stepping into the transformative journey of parenthood for the first time or are bravely navigating the complexities of fertility challenges, these 40 days are designed to be a sacred space where God's Word can speak directly to your heart. Here, you are invited to declare His timeless promises and prepare your spirit to embrace the blessing of new life.

Within each daily meditation, you will find thoughtfully selected scriptures, heartfelt prayers, and empowering confessions that together build a resilient foundation for your family and deepen your trust in God's perfect plan. Every day's devotion offers you a quiet sanctuary to reflect, release, and recharge, enabling you to draw strength and encouragement from His eternal truths. We encourage you to hold each other's hands when praying the prayers and also when declaring the confessions. The scriptures say in Matthew 18:19 that if two of you agree on earth about anything they ask, it will be done for them by my Father in heaven.

As you travel this path, know that you are not walking alone; we are praying alongside you, united in expectation and faith. May each page fill you with joy and inspire a profound trust in the divine purpose mapped out for you. We are eagerly waiting for the moment when your journey transitions into celebration, witnessing the fulfilment of promises that have sustained your hope.

May this devotional be a beacon of light and love, guiding you through this precious season and always reminding you that, with God, every promise carried forth leads to a miracle fulfilled.

DAY 1

EMBRACING THE BLESSING MANDATE: BE FRUITFUL & MULTIPLY

VERSE OF THE DAY

Then God blessed them, and God said to them, "Be fruitful and multiply; fill the earth and subdue it; have dominion over the fish of the sea, over the birds of the air, and over every living thing that moves on the earth." (Genesis 1:28, NKJV)

REFLECTION

God's first command to humanity was to flourish and grow, a promise rooted in His creative power. He declared, "Be fruitful and multiply." Fruitfulness is not an afterthought; it is embedded in creation's DNA. While circumstances may scream barrenness, Heaven still echoes that inaugural decree. Whether you are eagerly anticipating your first child or holding onto hope after a season of waiting, know that you are part of a legacy of fruitfulness. Embrace this call as an opportunity to cultivate an environment where faith, love, and hope flourish. Be confident that the God who spoke it will empower it.

PRAYER

Father, thank You for pronouncing fruitfulness over us from the beginning. We receive that blessing afresh and invite Your creative life into every part of our lives. With great expectations, we receive the empowerment to walk boldly into Your plan for fruitfulness and guide us as we prepare for our babies. Fill our spirits with the assurance of Your promises and inspire us to trust in Your perfect timing.

CONFESSIONS

- We declare that our home is a sanctuary of love and abundant blessings, a garden God ordained for life and increase.

- My (wife's) womb is blessed to receive, nurture and deliver healthy children.

- We affirm that God is orchestrating a future filled with hope and divine purpose.

JOURNAL: WHAT IS GOD SAYING?

Created in His Image:
A Calling for Fruitfulness

VERSE OF THE DAY

"So God created human beings in his own image. In the image of God he created them; male and female he created them" (Genesis 1:27, NLT)

REFLECTION

We are created in the image of God, a calling that brings honour and responsibility. Being image-bearers means we mirror the God who creates and cultivates. Infertility is not our identity. As you wait for your child, remember that you reflect His glory. Your journey into parenthood is a testimony of God's creative power and His desire to see His image carried forward. Every word you speak, every prayer you utter, shapes the destiny of your family. Today, let your heart be filled with the understanding that your future child will carry the imprint of God's image, a living legacy of His love and purpose. Today, reject labels of barrenness and embrace the dignity and authority that comes from being handcrafted by God. Trust in God's faithful promise, and know that you will carry your children.

PRAYER

Heavenly Father, we thank You for making us in Your image. As we wait for the gift of our babies, help us to reflect Your glory in every word and deed. Let Your likeness within us overthrow every message of limitation. May our children reflect Your beauty and purpose.

CONFESSIONS

- We declare that our marriage displays God's creative brilliance.

- We speak and declare that life, purpose and favour flow through us to the next generation.

- We affirm that our children will shine and radiate God's image in Jesus Name.

JOURNAL: WHAT IS GOD SAYING?

DAY 3

TRUSTING IN GOD'S PERFECT TIMING

VERSE OF THE DAY

"He has set the right time for everything"
(Ecclesiastes 3:1, GNT)

REFLECTION

Waiting can be challenging, but we understand that God's timing is flawless. In every season of anticipation, it is essential to learn to trust that every delay is part of the grand design of God. God writes stories with perfect pacing. Waiting is not a waste; it is woven. You are to remember that just as the seasons change in nature, your lives are being prepared for something beautiful.

PRAYER

God of all seasons, we place our waiting into Your capable hands and we surrender our calendar to You. Teach us to trust Your perfect timing and to embrace every season with hope. Teach us to see time as Your servant, and not our enemy. Help us to cultivate patience and joy while we wait in Jesus Name.

CONFESSIONS

- We declare that we trust in God's timing in every season of our lives.

- We speak forth peace, hope and perseverance as we await His blessings.

- We affirm that every moment of waiting is a stepping stone to divine purpose.

JOURNAL: WHAT IS GOD SAYING?

DAY 4

EMBRACING THE GIFT OF HOPE

VERSE OF THE DAY

"For I know the plans I have for you,' says the Lord. 'They are plans for good and not for disaster, to give you a future and a hope" (Jeremiah 29:11, NLT)

REFLECTION

Hope is a precious gift embedded in God's promises. It is God's lifeline in our waiting season. God's plans promise prosperity and joy, even when the path feels uncertain. As you journey through your waiting season, cling to the assurance that your future is bright and full of promise. Even when the road seems uncertain, this promise reassures you that every moment is part of a greater tapestry that leads to joy, abundance, and the fulfilment of His Word. Let hope be your steady companion as you speak life into your future.

PRAYER

Dear Lord, we thank You for the gift of hope. As we wait, fill our hearts with the promise of a prosperous future. Help us to live in anticipation of Your loving plans and to share that hope with those around us.

- We declare that hope fills our hearts and guides our steps.

- We speak of a future of joy and prosperity for our family. A future glowing with God's goodness.

- We affirm that God's plans for our family are full of hope and divine assurance.

JOURNAL: WHAT IS GOD SAYING?

DAY 5

BUILDING A GODLY FOUNDATION

VERSE OF THE DAY

"Unless the Lord builds a house, the work of the builders is wasted" (Psalm 127:1, NLT)

REFLECTION

A strong family begins with a solid foundation built on God's Word. As you prepare for parenthood, invest time in nurturing your relationship with God and with one another. Let your home be a sanctuary where His love reigns and His truth guides every decision. Today, commit to building your family on the firm foundation of faith, ensuring that every stone is set in love, prayer, and divine purpose. May your home become a sanctuary of love and faith where every brick is laid in honour of His truth.

PRAYER

Lord, we invite You to be the cornerstone of our family. As we build our future, guide our decisions and fill our home with Your love. Empower us to lay a foundation that will stand firm for generations to come.

CONFESSIONS

- We declare that our home is built on the unshakeable foundation of God's Word.

- We speak forth unity, love and strength over every aspect of our family.

- We affirm that our future is secured in the hands of the Almighty.

JOURNAL: WHAT IS GOD SAYING?

Confessing Blessings for Our Future Children

VERSE OF THE DAY

"He gives the childless woman a family, making her a happy mother. Praise the LORD!" (Psalm 113:9, NLT)

REFLECTION

Your child is not merely an addition to your family; they are a divine gift. Today, take a moment to confess blessings over the lives that are being formed. Picture the unique personality, gifts, and calling that God has designed for your future children. As you speak these blessings, remember that every word has power. Your faith-filled declarations can shape a destiny and invite God's favour into the lives of your children.

PRAYER

Heavenly Father, we thank You for the promise of new life. Guide us to speak blessings into every moment as we prepare to welcome our children. Strengthen us to be faithful stewards of Your gifts and to nurture our future children with love and thanksgiving.

CONFESSIONS

- I declare that the womb of my wife (wife: my womb) is blessed and will carry our babies.

- We speak forth that all our reproductive organs are functioning properly in accordance with God's design.

- We affirm that our hands shall carry our children and that we receive our children with thanksgiving.

JOURNAL: WHAT IS GOD SAYING?

DAY 7

SURRENDERING TO GOD'S PLAN

VERSE OF THE DAY

"Trust in the LORD with all your heart and lean not on your own understanding." (Proverbs 3:5, NKJV)

REFLECTION

Surrender is not about giving up; it's about trusting that God's plan surpasses our own ideas. In moments of uncertainty, remind yourself that God sees the full picture. As you wait, let your heart rest in the truth that He is orchestrating every detail. Surrendering your worries and doubts to Him allows you to receive His peace and direction, paving the way for a future filled with His goodness.

PRAYER

Lord, we surrender our fears and uncertainties to You. Strengthen our trust and help us to lean fully on Your understanding. Guide our steps as we walk in obedience to Your perfect plan for our family.

CONFESSIONS

- We declare that we surrender fully to God's divine plan.

- We speak forth trust, obedience and peace over our hearts.

- We affirm that God's understanding exceeds our own and that we walk confidently in His purpose.

JOURNAL: WHAT IS GOD SAYING?

DAY 8

Nurturing a Spirit of Patience

VERSE OF THE DAY

"But if we hope for what we do not see, we wait eagerly for it with patience and composure." (Romans 8:25, MSG)

REFLECTION

Patience is a vital ingredient in the waiting season. It's a testament to your faith that you trust in God's promises even before they manifest. Today, focus on cultivating a spirit of patience, one that believes, waits, and remains expectant. Remember, every moment of waiting is a building block toward the lives that God are preparing for you. Embrace this season, knowing that it is part of a journey that is both transformative and blessed.

PRAYER

Lord, help us to nurture a spirit of patience and to trust in Your perfect timing. Infuse our hearts with perseverance and encourage us to wait with joyful expectation. Let every day be a testament to Your unending love.

CONFESSIONS

- We declare that we embrace patience and trust in God's process.

- We speak forth growth in resilience and hopeful expectation in every moment of waiting.

- We affirm that our hearts are filled with calm assurance as we anticipate God's blessings.

JOURNAL: WHAT IS GOD SAYING?

DAY 9

PREPARING OUR HEARTS FOR PARENTHOOD

VERSE OF THE DAY

"Start children off on the way they should go, and even when they are old they will not turn from it." (Proverbs 22:6, NIV)

REFLECTION

Parenthood is not merely a role; it's a calling to guide a life in the ways of the Lord. As you prepare for this journey, take time to ready your heart and mind for the responsibilities and joys ahead. Reflect on the legacy you wish to build, a home where faith is not just taught but lived. Today, commit to cultivating spiritual habits that will one day be the foundation for your child's walk with God.

PRAYER

Lord, prepare our hearts as we await the gift of parenthood. Grant us wisdom, compassion and strength to nurture the life You are preparing. Help us to lead by example and to create a home where Your truth is lived every day.

CONFESSIONS

- We declare that our hearts are prepared to guide our future child in God's ways.

- We speak forth wisdom, love and integrity over our family.

- We affirm that our hearts are ready to nurture a legacy of faith and honour.

JOURNAL: WHAT IS GOD SAYING?

DAY 10

STEADFAST HOPE
AMID BAD NEWS

VERSE OF THE DAY

"They do not fear bad news; they confidently trust the Lord to care for them. They are confident and fearless …...."
(Psalm 112:7-8, NLT)

REFLECTION

Waiting seasons can test your spirit, especially when bad news strikes, whether it's a disheartening medical report, a negative remark from a family member, or criticism from someone you trust. These moments can feel like foes rising against you, threatening to steal your hope. Yet, we are called to a higher place: a life free from the fear of bad news. This isn't denial, it's a choice to trust God's care above all else. When the doctor's words sting or a loved one's doubt echoes in your mind, you're encouraged to stand confident and fearless. Why? Because your foundation isn't in fleeting reports or opinions, it's in the Lord who cares for you. You can rise above negativity, not by your own strength, but by trusting in God's unchanging goodness.

PRAYER

Lord, we lift our hearts to You in this waiting season. When unpleasant news or negative words come our way, anchor us in Your truth. Help us trust You with unwavering confidence, free from fear. Strengthen us to rise above every foe, doubt, discouragement, or despair, and fill us with Your peace. Thank You for caring for us, even in the hardest moments.

CONFESSIONS

- We declare that we will not fear unpleasant news; our trust is in the Lord's faithful care.

- We speak forth with confidence and fearlessness, we stand strong in the Lord.

- We affirm that we rise above negativity and face every challenge with triumph through Christ.

JOURNAL: WHAT IS GOD SAYING?

DAY 11

The Power of Faith in Fertility Challenges

VERSE OF THE DAY

"Not one promise from God is empty of power, for nothing is impossible with God." (Luke 1:37, TPT)

REFLECTION

For those facing fertility challenges, every day can be a test of faith. Today, remind yourself that faith is not the absence of difficulty but the assurance that God is bigger than every obstacle. In moments of discouragement, remember that Jesus declared all things possible for those who believe. Your journey is a testament to perseverance, and every prayer is a step toward the breakthrough that God has in store

PRAYER

Lord Jesus, we come before You with hearts full of belief. Strengthen our faith as we overcome every challenge and help us to trust that all things are possible through You. Inspire us to walk boldly in Your promises as we await the miracle of our babies.

CONFESSIONS

- We declare that our faith is unyielding and that every challenge is met with divine strength.

- We speak forth the power of God in every aspect of our journey.

- We affirm that our bodies receive wholeness and that every reproductive system functions in perfect alignment with God's will.

JOURNAL: WHAT IS GOD SAYING?

DAY 12

WALKING IN DIVINE CONFIDENCE

VERSE OF THE DAY

"So do not throw away this confident trust in the Lord. Remember the great reward it brings you! Patient endurance is what you need now, so that you will continue to do God's will. Then you will receive all that he has promised"
(Hebrews 10:35-36, NLT)

REFLECTION

Confidence in God's promises is a powerful tool in the waiting season. As you walk this path, let divine confidence fill your spirit, dispelling any shadow of doubt. Remember that your journey is seen and orchestrated by a loving God who delights in blessing those who trust in Him. Each step you take is supported by His strength and the assurance that His promises never fail.

PRAYER

Father, help us to walk in divine confidence. Remove any doubts and replace them with unwavering trust in Your promises. Empower us to boldly speak truth and hope over my family, confident that Your blessings are on the way. Amen.

CONFESSIONS

- We declare that we walk boldly in confidence because God is our steadfast guide.

- We speak forth the strength and unwavering assurance of God over every day of our waiting.

- We affirm that divine favour surrounds our family and that our future is bright in God's light.

JOURNAL: WHAT IS GOD SAYING?

Healing Through His Word

VERSE OF THE DAY

"God spoke the words 'Be healed,' and we were healed, ..." (Psalm 107:20, TPT).

REFLECTION

God's voice alone has the power to heal and restore. Waiting season can feel like a wilderness, but Psalm 107:20 reminds us that God's word cuts through that wilderness with surgical precision. When He speaks, "Be healed," it's not just a wish, it's a command that reshapes reality. His word can mend the hidden wounds of longing, restore peace to a restless heart, and renew strength for the journey ahead. God has spoken "Be healed" over your body, your soul, and your future family. Trust that His word is working, even now, to bring you into the fullness of His plan.

PRAYER

Lord God, Your word declares healing and life, and we stand on that promise today. We bring before You our bodies, asking for Your restorative touch. Heal every part of us; our reproductive systems, our hormones, our health that needs alignment with Your design for fruitfulness. Where there is brokenness, speak "Be healed." Where there is delay, bring forth life.

- We declare that God's word brings healing and life to our bodies and our journey.

- We speak His promises of wholeness and fruitfulness over our future family.

- We affirm that His command delivers us from every fear and obstacle.

JOURNAL: WHAT IS GOD SAYING?

OUR BODY IS THE TEMPLE OF GOD

VERSE OF THE DAY

"Have you forgotten that your body is now the sacred temple of the Spirit of Holiness, who lives in you? You don't belong to yourself any longer, for the gift of God, the Holy Spirit, lives inside your sanctuary." (1 Corinthians 6:19, TPT)

REFLECTION

As believers, because we belong to Christ, our bodies are no longer our own; they are God's sanctuary, set apart for His purpose and glory. This is a reality that reshapes how we see ourselves. Jesus' sacrifice on the cross secured this truth for us. His body was broken so that ours would not have to be. No one pays for a crime twice. Jesus paid the full price for our sins, once and for all. Through His sacrifice, we are redeemed, and our bodies are made perfect and whole in God's sight. This wholeness extends to every part of us, including our physical health and even our hopes for new life.

PRAYER

Lord Jesus, thank You for paying the complete price for our perfect bodies through Your sacrifice on the cross. Help us to understand and cherish the truth that our bodies are Your temple. We ask for Your healing and blessing over our reproductive health. Strengthen our faith as we wait on You, trusting that You are preparing us for the gift of new life. May we live in the freedom and peace of Your finished work. Amen.

CONFESSIONS

- We declare that our bodies are the temple of God and they are not broken in Jesus name.

- We speak that our reproductive organs and hormones are perfect and balanced, functioning as God intended.

- We affirm that through Jesus' sacrifice, we are whole and aligned with God's promises for our lives.

JOURNAL: WHAT IS GOD SAYING?

RESTORED BY HIS HEALING POWER

VERSE OF THE DAY

"For I will restore health unto thee, and I will heal thee of thy wounds, saith the Lord" (Jeremiah 30:17, KJV)

REFLECTION

This period can feel like a wound, whether it's the physical challenge of infertility or the emotional strain of unanswered prayers. Yet, God declares that He will restore health to every part of your bodies, breathing life into places that feel barren and renewing your strength for the road ahead. This restoration is holistic, touching your physical health, your emotional resilience, and your spiritual hope. As you stand on this promise, picture God's hand at work, mending what's been wounded and preparing you for the fulfilment of His plan. This might mean a womb made ready; perfect reproduction organs, being restored to how God created them to function.

PRAYER

Lord, restore health to every part of our bodies, bring healing to every organ responsible for our reproduction, strengthen our weary hearts, and peace to our minds. As we wait for the blessing of our children, grant us patience to trust Your timing and faith to believe in Your power. We thank You that Your word never fails, and we rest in the assurance that You are making all things new. Amen.

CONFESSIONS

- We declare that the Lord is restoring health to every part of our bodies in Jesus name.

- We speak healing and fertility into my wife's (my) womb by the authority of God's word.

- We affirm that God's healing power is flowing through us, making us whole.

JOURNAL: WHAT IS GOD SAYING?

DAY 16

GROWING THROUGH TRIALS: TRUST IN THE PROCESS

VERSE OF THE DAY

*"Consider it a sheer gift, friends, when tests and challenges come...
Let it do its work so you become mature and well-developed..."*
(James 1:2-4, MSG)

REFLECTION

Trials are not setbacks; they help to refine and strengthen us. Trials refine, building the foundations for future blessings. They are stepping stones on the path of growth and deeper faith. As you wait for the fulfilment of God's promises, remember that each challenge refines you, prepares you, and draws you closer to His heart. Embrace the lessons learned in the waiting, knowing that every trial is a part of a process that is building you up for the blessings to come.

PRAYER

Lord, help us to see every trial as a stepping stone to a greater blessing. Strengthen our hearts and teach us to trust in Your refining process. Empower us to grow through every challenge and to rejoice in the lessons learned along the way.

- We declare that we grow stronger with every trial and that our faith is deepening by the day.

- We speak forth resilience, hope and strength over our journey of life.

- We affirm that our lives are being transformed for the better as we trust in God's process.

JOURNAL: WHAT IS GOD SAYING?

DAY 17

SUFFICIENT GRACE IN WAITING

VERSE OF THE DAY

"But he said to me, 'My grace is sufficient for you, for my power is made perfect in weakness.' Therefore, I will boast all the more gladly of my weaknesses, so that the power of Christ may rest upon me." (2 Corinthians 12:9, ESV)

REFLECTION

Waiting can often feel like an endless stretch of uncertainty, testing our patience and resolve. Yet, we know that God's grace is sufficient, especially when we feel weak. This isn't a call to grit our teeth and push through; it's an invitation to rest in His provision. When the days grow long and the prayers seem unanswered, His grace steps in, not as a mere consolation, but as a powerful force that thrives in our fragility. It's in those moments of surrender that we discover His strength holding us up. His grace doesn't just patch us up; it transforms our waiting into a testimony of His perfect strength. So, as you navigate this season, let His grace be your anchor.

PRAYER

Father, we come to You in our waiting, trusting in Your sufficient grace. When we feel weak and weary, lift our eyes to see Your power at work in us. Teach us to rejoice in our limitations, confident that Your strength is perfected there. Surround us with Your peace and sustain us with Your love.

CONFESSIONS

- We declare that God's grace is sufficient for us, meeting us in every moment of our waiting.

- We speak joy and strength over our weaknesses, knowing they reveal the power of Christ in our lives.

- We affirm that we are carried by His strength, trusting His grace to lead us through this journey.

JOURNAL: WHAT IS GOD SAYING?

ALIGNING OUR VISION WITH GOD'S VISION

VERSE OF THE DAY

"Write the vision; make it plain on tablets, so he may run who reads it." (Habakkuk 2:2, NIV)

REFLECTION

Our personal dreams and God's grand design are meant to work together. Today, take time to reflect on your desires, your hopes for your future child(ren), and your aspirations for a home filled with faith. As you speak and write down your vision, invite God to mould it into something that honours Him. When our hearts are aligned with His, our dreams become part of a larger, divine narrative.

PRAYER

Lord, we invite You to refine our vision and align it with Your divine plan. Grant us clarity, wisdom and purpose as we write our dreams in Your Word. Empower us to walk boldly in the path You have set before us.

CONFESSIONS

- We declare that our vision for our family is perfectly aligned with God's purpose.

- We speak forth a future filled with faith, hope and divine direction.

- We affirm that every step we take is guided by God's inspired vision.

JOURNAL: WHAT IS GOD SAYING?

DAY 19

DECLARING GOD'S BLESSINGS OVER YOUR HOME

VERSE OF THE DAY

"Every good and perfect gift is from above."
(James 1:17, NIV)

REFLECTION

Our home is the place where God's blessings come to life. Today, speak aloud the blessings that you want to see flourish in your family and home. Whether it's love, unity, joy, or peace, declare that these gifts are abundantly present in your home. When you declare God's goodness, you create an atmosphere where miracles happen and His love overflows.

PRAYER

Lord, we thank You for every good and perfect gift You bestow. Bless our home with love, unity and abundant joy. Guide us to declare Your goodness in every corner of our lives.

CONFESSIONS

- We declare that our home is filled with God's love and abundant blessings.

- We speak forth unity, joy and divine favour to saturate every area of our lives.

- We affirm that our household is a sanctuary of hope and lasting blessing.

JOURNAL: WHAT IS GOD SAYING?

DAY 20

PRAYERFUL EXPECTATION

VERSE OF THE DAY

"Therefore I tell you, whatever you ask for in prayer, believe that you have received it, and it will be yours." (Mark 11:24, NIV)

REFLECTION

Prayer is our channel for receiving the miraculous. Expect the extraordinary as you engage in prayer. Today, approach God with a heart full of expectation. Know that every prayer spoken in faith sets the stage for the miraculous. As you speak your desires out loud, let your heart be steadfast in believing that God hears and answers your every request. Let prayer become not just a habit, but a declaration of faith in what is to come and be established.

PRAYER

Lord, we come before You with expectant hearts. Ignite our faith and help us to pray with bold conviction. Empower us to believe that every prayer is answered and that our desires are already on the path to fulfilment.

- We declare that our prayers are powerful and effective.

- We speak forth expectation, faith and divine breakthrough over our lives.

- We affirm that we have received every promised blessing in the heart of faith.

JOURNAL: WHAT IS GOD SAYING?

DAY 21

BUILDING A
LEGACY OF FAITH

VERSE OF THE DAY

"And these words which I command you today shall be in your heart. You shall teach them diligently to your children..." (Deuteronomy 6:6-7, NKJV)

REFLECTION

Your future child(ren) is not just a blessing, they are a legacy. Today, consider the kind of legacy you want to leave behind: a legacy steeped in faith, hope, and unwavering trust in God. Every word you speak and every decision you make contributes to the spiritual heritage of your family. Embrace this calling to build a legacy that will influence generations to come. Prayerfully develop your family constitution and the legacy your family will be known for today.

PRAYER

Lord, help us to build a legacy of faith that our children will inherit. Strengthen our commitment to living in Your truth and guide us as we nurture our future generation. Empower us to lead by example and create a heritage of love and faith.

CONFESSIONS

- We declare that our lives are a foundation for a lasting legacy of faith.

- We speak forth enduring love, wisdom and spiritual guidance over our family.

- We affirm that our actions today plant seeds that will flourish for generations.

JOURNAL: WHAT IS GOD SAYING?

DAY 22

CULTIVATING A GRATEFUL HEART

VERSE OF THE DAY

"Give thanks in all circumstances; for this is God's will for you in Christ Jesus." (1 Thessalonians 5:18, NIV)

REFLECTION

Gratitude transforms our perspective and opens our hearts to even more blessings. As you wait, choose to be thankful for every small victory, every answered prayer, and every lesson learned. A grateful heart is a magnet for divine favour. Today, focus on the abundance already present in your life and let that gratitude shine through every word and action.

PRAYER

Lord, teach us to be grateful in every circumstance. Fill our hearts with joy and thankfulness as we receive Your endless blessings. Help us to reflect gratitude in every action and word as we walk in Your light.

CONFESSIONS

- We declare that our hearts overflow with gratitude for all of God's blessings.

- We speak forth thanksgiving, joy and praise over every moment of our lives.

- We affirm that gratitude opens the door to even greater favour and abundance.

JOURNAL: WHAT IS GOD SAYING?

Trusting the Unseen: Faith Over Fear

VERSE OF THE DAY

"For we live by faith, not by sight."
(2 Corinthians 5:7, NKJV)

REFLECTION

The unseen is where faith takes root. The waiting season can be shadowed by fears and uncertainties, but faith invites us to trust what we cannot see. Today, choose faith over fear. Remember that every promise of God is sure, even when your eyes can't yet see the fulfilment. Embrace the mystery of the unseen with confidence, knowing that the Creator of the universe is actively working in your life.

PRAYER

Lord, help us to see beyond what our eyes can discern. Strengthen our faith to overcome every fear and guide us to trust in Your unseen hand at work. Empower us to walk boldly in Your promises with hearts full of hope.

CONFESSIONS

- We declare that we live by faith and not by sight.

- We speak forth courage and trust to replace every fear in the midst of uncertainty.

- We affirm that God's promises shine brightly even in the unseen realms of our lives.

JOURNAL: WHAT IS GOD SAYING?

Preparing for a Fruitful Future

VERSE OF THE DAY

"But the fruit of the Spirit is love, joy, peace, forbearance, kindness, goodness, faithfulness, gentleness and self-control."
(Galatians 5:22-23, NIV)

REFLECTION

Your future is a garden waiting to be nurtured. Today, reflect on the fruit you wish to see in your family, qualities that speak of God's character. As you prepare for the arrival of your child(ren), allow the Spirit to cultivate love, joy, peace, and all the fruits that will define your home. Each spoken word of faith is like planting a seed that, in God's time, will blossom into a testimony of His goodness.

PRAYER

Lord, fill our hearts with the fruit of Your Spirit. Empower us to sow seeds of love, joy and peace in every aspect of our lives. Help us to nurture a future that blossoms with the beauty of God's divine purpose.

- We declare that our future is abundant and overflows with the fruit of the Spirit.

- We speak forth love, joy, peace and kindness over our journey.

- We affirm that every seed of faith we plant grows into a testament of God's blessing.

JOURNAL: WHAT IS GOD SAYING?

A Joyful Stirring: Our Baby is Leaping

VERSE OF THE DAY

"At the sound of Mary's greeting, Elizabeth's child leaped within her, and Elizabeth was filled with the Holy Spirit." (Luke 1:41, NLT)

REFLECTION

When Mary greeted Elizabeth, the baby leapt; a burst of joy that transcended the ordinary, signalling the nearness of the Saviour. For waiting parents, this moment is a powerful encouragement. It whispers that the life you're anticipating is already part of God's story, alive with purpose and ready to leap at the sound of His promise. As you wait for your child(ren), the Spirit is with you too, stirring hope, igniting faith, and breathing life into your journey.

PRAYER

Heavenly Father, thank You for the life that stirs even in the waiting. Like Elizabeth, fill us with Your Holy Spirit, awakening us to the joy and promise You're weaving into our story. We trust that You see the life we long for, and we ask for strength to believe in Your timing. Let us feel the leap of hope within us, a sign of Your nearness.

CONFESSIONS

- We declare that the baby is leaping in my wife's (my) womb, alive with God's purpose.

- We speak joy and divine life over our family's future.

- We affirm that the Holy Spirit fills us with hope and prepares us for our child.

JOURNAL: WHAT IS GOD SAYING?

DAY 26

ENVISIONING THE CHILD GOD HAS PLANNED

VERSE OF THE DAY

"You made all the delicate, inner parts of my body and knit me together in my mother's womb. Thank you for making me so wonderfully complex! Your workmanship is marvelous..." (Psalm 139:13-14, NLT)

REFLECTION

Your future child is a masterpiece in progress, a unique creation designed for good works. Today, take time to visualize the life that God is crafting for your little one. Envision a child who grows in wisdom, strength, and grace; a child who will make a difference in this world. Let your confessions and prayers today be filled with anticipation and gratitude for the unique purpose that awaits.

PRAYER

Lord, thank You for designing a beautiful future for our family. Open our eyes to see the potential in every moment and guide us as we prepare to nurture our child according to Your perfect will. Empower us to celebrate the miracle that is yet to come.

- We declare that our future child is fearfully and wonderfully made.

- We speak forth a destiny of purpose, hope and divine favour over our life.

- We affirm that our family is prepared to nurture and celebrate the miracle of new life (lives).

JOURNAL: WHAT IS GOD SAYING?

DAY 27

Faithful Affirmations: Speaking Life

VERSE OF THE DAY

"Death and life are in the power of the tongue."
(Proverbs 18:21, NKJV)

REFLECTION

Words have the power to shape destinies. As you prepare for parenthood, be intentional about the affirmations you speak over your future. Each word, when anchored in God's truth, becomes a seed that blossoms into life. Today, commit to speaking declarations that uplift, inspire, and activate God's promises in your home. Your voice is a tool for blessing; use it wisely.

PRAYER

Lord, empower our words to be instruments of life and blessing. Help us to speak truth with boldness and to declare Your promises over every situation. May our affirmations inspire hope and ignite transformation in our hearts.

CONFESSIONS

- We declare that our words carry the power to create life and abundance.

- We speak forth vibrant affirmations of hope, faith and divine purpose over our family.

- We affirm that every spoken word aligns with the truth of Your Word and brings forth Your promise.

JOURNAL: WHAT IS GOD SAYING?

DAY 28

PEACE IN THE WAITING

VERSE OF THE DAY

"Do not be anxious about anything, but in everything by prayer and supplication with thanksgiving let your requests be made known to God. And the peace of God, which surpasses all understanding, will guard your hearts and your minds in Christ Jesus" (Phil. 4:6-7, ESV)

REFLECTION

Waiting for a child can stir waves of anxiety, as the heart wrestles with uncertainty and longing. Instead of being consumed by worry, we are invited to bring every hope and concern to God through prayer, supplication, and thanksgiving. We are to lay down fears about the future and trust God with the desires of our heart. By presenting your requests with gratitude, you open the door to a supernatural peace that guards your mind and spirit, anchoring you in Christ's love even when the wait feels heavy. This peace, which surpasses understanding, is not a fleeting feeling but a divine gift that stands watch over your heart.

PRAYER

Father, we come before You with our longing for a child, choosing to release anxiety and embrace Your peace. Thank You for hearing our prayers and for Your promise to guard our hearts. Fill us with Your peace that surpasses understanding, calming our fears and strengthening our faith as we wait for Your perfect plan to unfold.

CONFESSIONS

- We declare that we cast all anxiety on God, trusting Him all the way.

- We speak peace and life over my wife's womb (my womb), believing in God's promise.

- We affirm that God's peace guards our hearts and minds in Christ Jesus.

JOURNAL: WHAT IS GOD SAYING?

DAY 29

BEING STILL IN THE WAITING SEASON

VERSE OF THE DAY

"Be still, and know that I am God" (Psalm 46:10, ESV)

REFLECTION

In seasons of waiting, it's easy to feel restless, like time is slipping away or that we need to act to make things happen. But Psalm 46:10 offers a counterintuitive invitation: "Be still, and know that I am God." This stillness isn't about doing nothing; it's about trusting deeply. It's a call to pause the striving, silence the what-ifs, and rest in the unshakable truth that God is in charge. When we're waiting for answers, breakthroughs, or clarity, stillness can feel vulnerable. Yet, it's in this space that we discover God's nearness. He doesn't ask us to figure it all out; He asks us to know Him. As you wait, know that God is sovereign, and His timing is flawless. Being still is your act of faith, a declaration that you trust Him to move when the moment is right.

PRAYER

Father, I bring my waiting to You. Help me to be still when my heart wants to rush ahead. Show me Your presence in this pause, and let me feel Your peace that surpasses understanding. Strengthen my faith to know You are God over every detail of my life. Thank You for working in ways I cannot yet see.

- We declare that God's timing is perfect, and we trust His plan for us.

- We speak forth that our stillness brings us closer to His heart and His will.

- We affirm that God is our refuge and we rest in His unchanging love.

JOURNAL: WHAT IS GOD SAYING?

DAY 30

A Time for Renewal and Hope

VERSE OF THE DAY

"See, I am doing a new thing! Now it springs up; do you not perceive it?" (Isaiah 43:19, NIV)

REFLECTION

Each day in the waiting season is an opportunity for renewal, a fresh start filled with hope. Today, allow God's transformative power to flow over you, renewing your spirit and infusing your heart with joy. Every moment of waiting is a chance to let go of the past and embrace the new possibilities God is laying before you. Trust that as you renew your mind in His truth, your future will be filled with His glory.

PRAYER

Lord, renew our hearts and minds with the refreshing power of Your love. Help us to release every burden of yesterday and step confidently into the new life You have prepared for us. Empower us to rejoice in every fresh start and to live in the hope of Your promises.

- We declare that we are renewed by the power of Christ and that each day is a fresh beginning.

- We speak forth hope, joy and transformation in every moment of our lives.

- We affirm that God is continuously renewing our hearts and preparing a bright future.

JOURNAL: WHAT IS GOD SAYING?

DAY 31

Claiming Victory in God's Promises

VERSE OF THE DAY

"But thanks be to God! He gives us the victory through our Lord Jesus Christ." (1 Corinthians 15:57, NIV)

REFLECTION

In every challenge, there is victory when we stand on the promises of God. Today, take a moment to claim the victories that are already yours; over fear, doubt, and every obstacle that stands in the way of your blessing. God's promises are not empty words; they are declarations of triumph that echo throughout the ages. Let this truth empower you to speak victory over your future and to stand firm in the knowledge that God's plan is unstoppable.

PRAYER

Lord, we thank You for the victorious promises that resound in our lives. Empower us to claim each blessing as a testament to Your mighty works. Help us to celebrate every win and to boldly declare that our future is filled with triumph.

- We declare that our victory is secured through Jesus Christ and that every challenge is overcome by divine strength.

- We speak forth triumph and unshakeable faith over our lives.

- We affirm that our journey is marked by victory, grace and the abundant promises of God.

JOURNAL: WHAT IS GOD SAYING?

DAY 32

HOLDING ONTO
GOD'S PROMISES I

VERSE OF THE DAY

"Let us hold unswervingly to the hope we profess, for he who promised is faithful." (Hebrews 10:23, NIV)

REFLECTION

God's promises anchor us during life's storms. Reaffirming our commitment to His Word ensures unwavering hope amidst uncertainty. Today, remind yourself that every promise spoken in Scripture is a secure anchor for your soul. Whether it's the promise of a future, the blessing of a child, or the peace that surpasses all understanding, hold on tightly. Let this day be a reaffirmation of your commitment to trust in a faithful God who never fails.

PRAYER

Lord, help us to cling to Your promises in every circumstance. Strengthen our resolve to trust in Your faithfulness and to live in the hope of Your Word. Empower us to walk confidently knowing that You are always true.

- We declare that we hold firmly to God's promises no matter the circumstance.

- We speak forth unwavering hope and trust in the faithfulness of God's Word.

- We affirm that our lives and future are securely anchored in God's everlasting promises.

JOURNAL: WHAT IS GOD SAYING?

HOLDING ONTO GOD'S PROMISES II

VERSES OF THE DAY

"The Lord kept his word and did for Sarah exactly what he had promised." (Genesis 21:1, NLT)

"No woman will miscarry or be childless in your land" (Exodus 23:26, CSB)

REFLECTION

We can hold onto God's promises in every situation, for His word never fails. God fulfilled His promise to Sarah, granting her a child after years of waiting and doubt. In Exo. 23:26, we have a powerful and bold declaration by God that no woman will be childless in our land. God's promises are not mere words; they are His covenant with you, sealed by His unchanging nature. Hold fast, knowing He is working to bring His purpose to life in your family.

PRAYER

Father, we thank You for Your unbreakable promises. Just as You kept Your word to Sarah, we trust You to fulfill Your plans for our family. Speak life over my wife's (my) womb, Lord, and protect us from loss or barrenness, as You promised in Your word. Strengthen our hearts to hold onto Your truth, even in moments of doubt. Fill us with faith and peace as we wait for the joy of welcoming our child, confident that You are faithful.

CONFESSIONS

- We declare that God's promises for our family are coming to pass, just as He did for Sarah.

- We speak fruitfulness and life over my wife's (my) womb, free from miscarriage or barrenness.

- We affirm that God's word is alive in us, bringing forth His abundant blessings.

JOURNAL: WHAT IS GOD SAYING?

DAY 34

WALKING IN THE SPIRIT OF CONFIDENCE

VERSE OF THE DAY

"So we say with confidence, 'The Lord is my helper; I will not be afraid. What can mere mortals do to me?"
(Hebrews 13:6, NIV)

REFLECTION

Confidence in God's protection and guidance can transform your waiting into a journey of boldness. Today, walk in the spirit of divine confidence, knowing that no earthly challenge can diminish the power of God's love. Let every step be a declaration of trust, and let your heart be filled with the assurance that with the Lord as your helper, you are unstoppable.

PRAYER

Lord, fill us with divine confidence as we navigate every challenge. Help us to move forward boldly and to declare Your strength in every situation. Empower us to face each day with courage and to rely on Your unfailing support.

CONFESSIONS

- We declare that we walk in fearless confidence because the Lord is our helper.

- We speak forth bold courage and unstoppable determination over our journey.

- We affirm that God's strength enables us to overcome every obstacle.

JOURNAL: WHAT IS GOD SAYING?

BUILDING RESILIENCE THROUGH FAITH

VERSE OF THE DAY

"And we know that in all things God works for the good of those who love him…" (Romans 8:28, NIV)

REFLECTION

Resilience is born from a deep trust in God's purpose, even when the path is steep. Today, acknowledge that every twist and turn in your journey is crafting a resilient spirit within you. Challenges are not roadblocks but opportunities for growth. Let your faith be the foundation that carries you through every obstacle, knowing that God is working all things together for your good.

PRAYER

Lord, strengthen our spirit and build our resilience through every trial. Help us to trust that You work all things together for our good and to find comfort in Your eternal promise. Empower us to overcome adversity with steadfast faith.

CONFESSIONS

- We declare that our resilience is fortified by our unwavering faith in God.

- We speak forth strength, endurance and determination in every circumstance.

- We affirm that God is working for our good and that every challenge makes us stronger.

JOURNAL: WHAT IS GOD SAYING?

DAY 36

LISTENING TO GOD'S WHISPER

VERSE OF THE DAY

"And after the fire, there was the sound of a gentle whisper."
(1 Kings 19:12, NLT)

REFLECTION

In the midst of life's clamour, God speaks softly to our hearts. Today, make space in your heart to truly listen to His voice. Whether it's through Scripture, prayer, or the quiet stirrings of the Holy Spirit, allow His gentle guidance to direct your steps. This is a time to slow down, to be present, and to tune into the divine frequency that only a heart surrendered to God can hear.

PRAYER

Lord, quiet our minds and help us to hear Your gentle whisper. Teach us to recognise Your voice in the quiet moments and to respond with eager obedience. Empower us to follow Your guidance each day with humble hearts.

CONFESSIONS

- We declare that we are attentive to the quiet voice of God in our lives.

- We speak forth receptive hearts that listen and obey God's divine guidance.

- We affirm that God's whisper directs our steps and fills our lives with purpose.

JOURNAL: WHAT IS GOD SAYING?

DAY 37

STRENGTHENING OUR MARITAL BOND

VERSE OF THE DAY

"And over all these virtues put on love, which binds them all together in perfect unity." (Colossians 3:14, NIV)

REFLECTION

The foundation of every family is a strong, loving relationship between partners. Today, focus on nurturing and deepening your marital bond. In times of waiting, lean on each other, encourage one another, and speak words of affirmation. Let love be the glue that holds you together, making your relationship a testimony of God's grace and a beacon of hope for the future.

PRAYER

Heavenly Father, strengthen the bond between us. Help us to love one another unconditionally and to support each other through every season. Guide our relationship with Your wisdom and fill our home with unity and love.

CONFESSIONS

- We declare that our marriage is a sanctuary of love, unity and mutual respect.

- We speak forth harmony, understanding and a deep commitment to one another.

- We affirm that our relationship is blessed and guided by God's unending love.

JOURNAL: WHAT IS GOD SAYING?

DAY 38

A Home Filled with Joy and Anticipation

VERSE OF THE DAY

"May the God of hope fill you with all joy and peace as you trust in him…" (Romans 15:13, NIV)

REFLECTION

Your home is not just a physical space, it's a wellspring of joy, peace, and anticipation for what's to come. Today, envision a household where laughter abounds, love is in every corner, and hope is the atmosphere. Even as you wait, fill your home with an energy that celebrates the promise of new life. Your declarations of joy and peace set the stage for the arrival of a blessing that will transform your world.

PRAYER

Lord, fill our home with boundless joy and peace. Help us to create an atmosphere of anticipation and love where every corner reflects Your grace. Empower us to celebrate every moment with grateful hearts.

- We declare that our home is a sanctuary of joy, peace and divine favour.

- We speak forth a loving environment where hope and happiness flourish.

- We affirm that every room in our household overflows with the blessings of God.

JOURNAL: WHAT IS GOD SAYING?

DAY 39

Celebrating the Journey: Our Trust in God

VERSE OF THE DAY

"Now to him who is able to do immeasurably more than all we ask or imagine, according to his power that is at work within us…" (Ephesians 3:20, NIV)

REFLECTION

As you reflect on this journey, take a moment to celebrate how far you've come. Reflect on the progress of your faith, the confessions you have declared, and the deep trust you have placed in God's promises. This journey is not just about waiting, it's about growing, transforming, and preparing for a future that exceeds every expectation. Let this day be a joyful celebration of God's immeasurable power at work in your life and your future family.

PRAYER

Lord, we thank You for every step of our journey. Help us to continue walking in trust and joy as we celebrate Your immeasurable power at work in our lives. Empower us to embrace every new day with grateful hearts and eager anticipation.

- We declare that our journey is a celebration of God's abundant love and power.

- We speak forth gratitude, trust and unwavering faith in every moment.

- We affirm that our future is blessed beyond measure by His infinite grace.

JOURNAL: WHAT IS GOD SAYING?

DAY 40

THANKSGIVING FOR GOD'S FAITHFULNESS

VERSE OF THE DAY

"Give thanks to the LORD, for he is good; his love endures forever." (Psalm 107:1, NIV)

REFLECTION

On this final day, let your hearts overflow with gratitude for God's unwavering faithfulness. Today, we pause to celebrate His goodness, remembering every answered prayer and every moment of grace along your journey. Be united in gratitude, knowing that every season of waiting has prepared you for the blessings that lie ahead.

PRAYER

Lord, we lift our voices in thanksgiving for Your never-ending love and faithfulness. Thank You for guiding us through every season and for preparing our hearts to receive Your abundant blessings. Empower us to live each day in grateful celebration of Your grace.

CONFESSIONS

- We declare that our lives are a testimony to God's faithful love and abundant blessings.

- We speak forth thanksgiving and praise for every miracle and answered prayer.

- We affirm that our hearts rejoice in the goodness of the Lord, now and forever.

JOURNAL: WHAT IS GOD SAYING?

CLOSING THOUGHTS

As you embark on this 40-day devotional journey, we pray it serves as a lighthouse in the midst of uncertainty, illuminating your heart with renewed hope and unwavering faith. Each day, as you speak these confessions and meditate on God's Word, may you find your steps guided by divine wisdom, forging a resilient spirit anchored in the promises of God. These moments of devotion aim not only to prepare you for the incredible blessing of parenthood but to transform every corner of your being, fostering healing and the joyful anticipation of a future woven with faith.

Remember, you are not alone on this path; our hearts are intertwined with yours, rooting for you, believing with you, and praying alongside you. Embrace each day's prayer with expectancy, allowing your faith in God to flourish, grow, and deepen. May this journey become a tapestry of strength, hope, and unshakeable belief, ushering you into a season of fulfilment and joy. We have confidence that before long, the seeds of faith and perseverance planted throughout this journey will blossom into a vibrant reality, and we look forward to celebrating this new chapter of life with you.

As God walks with you on this precious journey, may His peace envelop you and His blessings overflow upon you and your family. May each day bring revelation, comfort, and delight, and may these reflections inspire not only today's hope but tomorrow's radiant assurance.

God bless you abundantly and keep you steadfast in His grace. We look forward to reading your beautiful testimonies of God's faithfulness and goodness.

NOTES

NOTES

NOTES